SIGHT-SING ANY MELODY
INSTANTLY

BY MARK PHILLIPS

Also available:

Sight-Read Any Rhythm Instantly, by Mark Phillips
(02500457)

ISBN 978-1-57560-514-2

Visit our website at www.cherrylane.com

INTRODUCTION

What Is Sight-Singing?

Practically every movie that depicts the life story of a famous songwriter contains a scene in which the composer hands a (usually female) singer a newly written song and says, "Try this." The singer then takes one look at the sheet of paper and bursts into song. What she's doing is known as *sight-singing*—the reading and simultaneous singing of an unfamiliar melody. Watching the film, you may wonder: *How does she do that?* After all, nobody has played the melody for her on an instrument, and there are no little valves on her neck (like those on a trumpet) that she can press to achieve the correct pitches.

If you've ever tried to learn sight-singing yourself, that type of Hollywood scene can be frustrating. How is it, you might ask, that the pretty singer in the movie, who probably doesn't have perfect pitch (most people don't) and who probably never even studied music theory, can sight-sing flawlessly when your own attempts have been, at best, hesitant and blundering?

One answer is that the movie is fictionalized. Most people (even sight-singing teachers) can't sight-sing as effortlessly as does the singer in that film. (And you know that the situation is bogus because in the middle of the song she continues singing even as she looks away from the sheet music to smile at the composer.) But a better answer is that it really is possible to sight-sing effortlessly—if you know the trick.

About This Book

Many people learn to sight-sing when they study music theory and ear-training in college. But many college programs are ineffective. I know of one university that doesn't teach their music majors any particular method of sight-singing; instead, the students are expected to somehow divine the correct pitches. Another school I know of does teach a method, but it's one (based on intervals) that doesn't work. (See Chapter 1 for an explanation of why the "interval" method is flawed.)

This book teaches you a sight-singing technique, or trick, that truly works. And the amazing thing is that—just as Dorothy had the ability to get back to Kansas all along (by clicking her heels together three times)—you've had the ability to sight-sing all along! If you doubt that, here's proof. Imagine that you're about to sing in front of a group of people. Say you're at a party and you've been asked to sing "Happy Birthday to You." Once the piano player establishes the key by giving you a short introduction, *you automatically hit the correct starting note.* And you didn't even have to think about it; the first note's pitch came effortlessly from within you. Wouldn't it be nice if sight-singing were that simple? Well, actually it is—because the crux of the technique that this book teaches is based entirely on something you already possess: a natural ability (once a key has been established) to correctly sing the first note of any well-known song (but more on this in Chapter 1).

Who Is This Book For?

This book is for anyone—college music majors, chorus members, professional singers—who wants to be able to look at a piece of written music and instantly sing it aloud. But it's also for anyone—conductors, instrumentalists, song publishers, music editors, arrangers—who wants to be able to look at written music and hear the sound of the notes in his head.

What You Need to Know to Use This Book

To use this book you need to know (1) how to read music, (2) how to determine what key a piece of music is in (by looking at the key signature), and (3) what degree of the scale (1, 2, 3, 4, 5, 6, or 7) any particular note in that key represents. If you can't read music, then this book is beyond your grasp. But even if you don't know how to determine keys or scale degrees, you can learn that by studying "Appendix B: Major and Minor Scales Identified by Letter Name and Scale Degree." By the way, the sight-singing exercises presented here contain no difficult or tricky rhythms. But if you need help with rhythmic reading, see my *Sight-Read Any Rhythm Instantly* (Cherry Lane Music, 02500457).

About the Music Examples

Anyone writing an instructional book on sight-singing must make certain decisions concerning such issues as keys and clefs. For example, does one write exercises in all 12 major and minor keys, or in only the more commonly used keys? And does one duplicate all treble clef examples in bass clef? For the sake of brevity and "user-friendliness," I wrote all the examples in common keys only (no more than four sharps or flats in the key signature) and in treble clef only (as more treble clef readers exist than do bass clef readers). But because the technique (or thought process) this book teaches applies to any key and any clef, you should have no trouble sight-singing music in less common keys or in bass clef. By the way, if you want to use this book to practice sight-singing in difficult keys or in bass clef, you can mentally change a key signature or clef, then simply sing the notes as written, but in the new key.

Whereas some sight-singing books present practice examples contrived by the author, this book features *actual songs* for you to sight-sing. Of course, if you were familiar with these songs, you'd be able to sing them from memory and they'd serve no instructional purpose. That's why I've chosen songs that, though they've stood the test of time, are not currently familiar. I haven't identified them by title (there's no reason to), but if you're curious, they come from a variety of musical realms: folk, classical, popular, patriotic, and international.

Now click your heels together three times and let's sing!

—Mark Phillips

CONTENTS

CHAPTER 1:
LEARNING "1," "3," AND "5"

Imagine that you're a singer onstage, ready to perform the first song of your set. Your accompanist plays a short introduction and you begin to sing. Bingo!—the first note out of your mouth is the correct pitch!

Now you're ready for your second song. Again the accompanist plays a short introduction and again you begin singing on the correct pitch!

How does that happen? After all, your piano player didn't provide you with a particular starting note; he simply played a chordal introduction. Well, your mind provided the correct pitch—and it did so effortlessly. And because you possess the natural ability to correctly sing the first note of any well-known song, you possess the ability to sight-sing!

The only reason you can't sight-sing now is simply that no one ever bothered to point out to you which degree of the scale (1, 2, 3, 4, 5, 6, or 7) any particular song begins on. What you'll learn here is which well-known songs begin on which scale degrees and how to use that information to sight-sing any melody instantly.

How does that work? Let's say you knew that the song "Twinkle, Twinkle, Little Star" happens to begin on the *first degree* of the scale. (You can prove this to yourself by going to an instrument and playing a C major scale and then playing the song in C, by ear; you'll see that it indeed begins on a C—the first degree of the C scale.) Now say that you're holding a piece of written music that begins on C and is in the key of C. All you have to do to correctly sight-sing that first note is *pretend* you're going to sing "Twinkle, Twinkle, Little Star," but sing only the *first note*. You'll automatically hit the correct pitch (just as when you were onstage with your imaginary piano player). And if you know other well-known songs that happen to begin on other scale degrees (2, 3, 4, 5, 6, and 7) you can use this "pretend you're going to sing the song but sing only the first note" technique to correctly and effortlessly sing any pitch you might encounter.

Hearing "1," "3," and "5"

In this chapter you'll learn which famous songs' starting notes correspond to the scale degrees "1," "3," and "5" (the easiest ones to hear), and you'll practice sight-singing melodies using those degrees.

By the way, as you become more proficient in sight-singing, you'll gradually *memorize* the sounds of the various scale degrees and thus be able to sing pitches automatically; that is, you won't actually have to go through the ordeal of pretending you're going to sing a famous song for every note you see. But for now, in order to first learn and work with these sounds, that's the technique you'll need to use. It's a four-step method: (1) determine the letter name of the pitch you want to sing, (2) determine the scale degree of that pitch (in the key of the music you'll be singing), (3) think of the famous song that begins on that pitch, (4) sing the first note of that song.

How, you might ask, can a four-step method become nearly instantaneous and automatic? By way of analogy, consider what happens when you retype text: you (1) look at the first letter you want to retype and determine what it is, (2) find that letter on the computer keyboard, (3) decide which finger you'll use to type the letter, (4) press down the key with that finger. You know, of course, that as you become proficient in typing, those four steps converge into one, and the process becomes effortless and automatic. With practice, you'll be able to achieve the same effortlessness in your sight-singing.

A word about establishing keys: Because you don't have perfect pitch, if you want to sing a piece of music in the key it's written in, you (or someone else) must establish the key (as by playing a few chords or scales on an in-tune instrument). "Appendix A: Establishing the Key (At Piano or Solo Instrument) for All Major and Minor Keys" contains short chordal phrases for piano and short scalar phrases for single-note instruments that, if played, will establish any key for you. On the other hand, since the thought process you're going to use here applies to any and all keys, you might not care if you're singing in the actual key of the written music—so long as all the notes you sing are correct relative to each other. If that's the case, feel free to pick any key that feels comfortable for your vocal range (and, not having perfect pitch, you won't even know what that key is), and simply *pre-*

tend you're singing in the written key (just as you might pretend that your home piano, which hasn't been tuned in five years, isn't really a half step flat).

Now let's learn the sound of "1." Many well-known songs begin on the first scale degree, or "1." Below I show the first two bars of four of them (all here in the key of C). Look at them; play them; listen to them.

Ex. 1-1

Do you hear how each song begins on the same note? "My," "I've," "Old," and "Twin-" are all C's; each represents the first scale degree ("1"). By the way, the technical term for the first scale degree is *tonic*. Go ahead and try out the technique: Sing a C by realizing that (in the key of C) it's the first scale degree (or tonic) and by pretending you're really going to sing one of these four songs. Do it; sing it.

Now that you have the idea, let's choose just *one* song (and its corresponding first syllable) for you to use to remember the sound of "1." We'll refer to it as "your song" for singing "1." It should be the song that works best for you. As we go along, you'll do this for each scale degree. But at the same time, for each scale degree, I will suggest what I think is a good song (and corresponding first syllable) to use, which I'll call "my suggestion." This way, as I speak of various scale degrees in terms of "first words of songs," as we go along, I'll have a particular syllable to refer to. And by all means, you may adopt "my suggestion" as "your song." (If you're curious, I've chosen "my suggestion" based on various factors, including how well the song is known, how easy the syllable is to vocalize, to what extent the song's first note helps reinforce the key you're in, etc.).

My suggested song for the tonic (first degree) is "My Country, 'Tis of Thee." No matter what key you're in, the tonic note will sound like that song's first note, the one you sing on the first syllable, "My." Now turn to the back of the book for a moment and take a look at "Appendix D: Famous Songs for Learning Each Scale Degree." You'll see a variety of songs that begin on "1." Looking them over, you might find one that works better for you than "My Country, 'Tis of Thee." Maybe "Over the Rainbow" or something else works best for you. Now go ahead and choose "your song."

For every scale degree, in addition to suggesting a famous song that begins on that degree, I'll present you with what I call a "special song." These "special songs" are not famous songs; in fact, they're not even songs. Each "special song" is a specially contrived short phrase that, once memorized as if it were a song, not only helps you remember the sound of a particular scale degree (as "My Country, 'Tis of Thee" does for "1"), but at the same time strongly reinforces the key (or scale) you're singing in. Why does the key need to be reinforced, and how does a "special song" reinforce it?

Every scale or key has one note that's considered "home base." It's the most important note in the scale or key, the one the scale or key is named after. But instead of being called "home," it's called "1" or "tonic." Whenever you sight-sing, the sound of the tonic must be in your mind, either consciously or semiconsciously. Sometimes that "tonic in your mind" is the single note that starts the scale; more often it's the sound and feeling of the entire key that's based on that starting note. In order for your sight-singing to be meaningful, each scale degree you sing must relate to *the same tonic.* And the only way that can happen is if the tonic is always in your mind.

Two ways to reinforce the tonic are (1) by singing or listening to the tonic note (first scale degree) and (2) by singing or listening to the *tonic triad.* The tonic triad is the three-note chord based on the tonic note. For example, in the key of C, the C note is the tonic note, and the C chord (or C major chord, or C major triad—namely, a chord made up of the notes C, E, and G) is the tonic triad. Nothing establishes or reinforces a key better than hearing that tonic note or chord.

Most of these "special songs" are short descending phrases that (1) begin on the note in question, (2) move down to the nearest member of the tonic triad, and (3) descend the triad, note by note, landing on "1" (or home), reinforcing the key. Don't try to learn or memorize the sounds of these "special songs" now, but for the purpose of illustration, here is what each of the seven "special songs" looks like, in terms of scale degrees: 1; 2–1; 3–1; 4–3–1, 5–3–1; 6–5–3–1; 7–8 (1). To use a water analogy, if you think of a particular starting note (of a "special song") as a tributary or stream, it flows down to the tonic triad "river," then flows down that river to the tonic lake (or bay or ocean)—"home." Nothing can stop the water in a tributary from naturally flowing down to the river and then down to the lake. Once you've memorized these seven "special songs," each scale degree will inevitably flow down, through your mind's tonic river (triad), to your mind's tonic lake (first scale degree or key center), *strongly reinforcing the key.*

Now let's memorize the sound of the "special song" for "1." As indicated above, it's simply one note—the tonic note. Establish the key of C for yourself and, with the sound of the key firmly in your mind, sing the "special song" a few times. It may feel silly to sing a song consisting of only one note, but go ahead and do it anyway. Sing "One . . . One . . . One."

Ex. 1 - 2

"One"

Admittedly, that wasn't much of a song, and in helping to reinforce the key, it had nowhere to "flow." But as we proceed to the higher scale degrees, you'll come to see that these "special songs" are quite effective in reinforcing the tonic. As a matter of fact, because they're so effective, if you like, you can use the "special songs" (rather than famous songs) as "your songs" for memorizing the sounds of the various scale degrees. But if you prefer to use famous songs as "your songs" (because you're already familiar with them), always learn and memorize the "special songs," too, as *second* "your songs." That way, you can always take a nice, restorative dip in the lake, so to speak.

Now let's learn the sound of "3." By the way, the technical name of the third scale degree is *mediant.* Below, in the key of C, are the first two bars of four famous songs that begin on scale degree "3." Play them; sing them.

Ex. 1-3

The First Noel

The— first— No - el...

Mary Had a Little Lamb

Mar - y had a lit - tle lamb...

Old Folks at Home (Swanee River)

Way down up - on the Swan - ee Riv - er...

Three Blind Mice

Three blind mice, three blind mice...

See how they all start on the same note—E or "3"? Learn the sound of "3" by pretending you're onstage about to sing one of these songs and that your piano player just finished playing an intro. Start to sing, but sing only the first note. There! You've just pulled "3" right out of the air.

My suggested song for "3" is "Swanee River" ("Way down upon the Swanee River"), so my suggested syllable is "Way." Now choose "your song." Don't forget to check out additional possibilities in Appendix D at the back.

Now here's the "special song" for "3." Play it; sing it; memorize it. Sing it over and over: "Three, one . . . Three, one . . . Three, one."

Ex. 1-4

"Three, one"

Below are the first two bars, in the key of C, of four famous songs that begin on "5." Play them; sing them. They all start on the same note, G—the fifth scale degree in the key of C. By the way, the technical term for the fifth scale degree is *dominant.*

Ex. 1-5

America the Beautiful

O   beau - ti - ful   for   spa - cious skies...

The Battle Hymn of the Republic

Mine eyes have seen the glo - ry of the com - ing of the Lord...

Deck the Halls

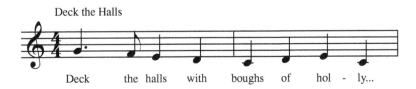

Deck   the halls   with   boughs   of   hol - ly...

The Star Spangled Banner

O——— say,   can   you   see...

Again, learn the sound by pretending you're going to sing one of these songs, but sing only the first note. My suggested song for "5" is "Deck the Halls." Now choose "your song" (don't forget to check out Appendix D).

Here's the "special song" for "5." Flow down the river to the sea by singing "Five, three, one . . . Five, three, one . . . Five, three, one."

Ex. 1-6

"Five,   three,   one"

Exercises Using "1," "3," and "5"

Before we sing any real songs, let's try a few exercises using "1," "3," and "5" in the key of C. By they way, we're starting off in the key of C because most people find this key the easiest to deal with. Maybe that's because on a piano keyboard the C scale involves only the white keys; in any case, C major generally serves as a starting point for theoretical discussions and practical exercises.

In Exs. 1-7 and 1-8 you'll see four layers of "lyrics" below the notes. Depending on how they're taught, different people use different systems for vocalizing when sight-singing. For example, some sing an ascending major scale by vocalizing "do, re, mi, fa, sol, la, ti, do"; others sing by numbers: "one, two, three, four, five, six, seven, eight"; and still others vocalize letter names: (in the key of C) "C, D, E, F, G, A, B, C."

Your aim here is to vocalize *numbers* when you sight-sing. Why? Because singing numbers always reinforces the key in your mind; that is, by singing numbers, you constantly verbalize the relationship between the note you're singing and the tonic. In Exs. 1-7 and 1-8, you've been given the letter name and scale degree of each note. Below that, for each note, is the syllable that corresponds to my suggested song, and below that is a blank where you can fill in the syllable that correspond to "your song." Now, here's your thought process for starting to sight-sing Ex. 1-7:

1. You look at the first note and see that it's a G.

2. You realize that in the key you're in (C), G represents "5."
3. You remember that "Deck the Halls" (or substitute "your song") begins on "5."
4. You begin to sing "Deck the Halls," but you sing only the first note.

Next, you move to the second note (C), and follow the same procedure; that is, realize C is "1," and pretend you're going to sing "My Country, 'Tis of Thee" (or "your song" for "1"), but sing only the first note. Then continue similarly through the entire example.

Because this is your first attempt at sight-singing with the "first note of a famous song" technique, you might find it easier to verbalize, for Ex. 1-7, the syllables "Deck, My, Way . . ." instead of "Five, One, Three . . ." because doing so involves one less step (that is, when you pretend to sing the famous song you'll actually sing that song's first syllable rather than a substituted number for that syllable). However, very quickly you'll need to give up that crutch and verbalize numbers instead of actual song lyrics. That's why in Ex. 1-9 you don't see any actual song lyrics under the notes.

Ex. 1-7

In Ex. 1-9 you're given only each note's letter name and scale degree. It's up to you to remember "your song" for each note. If you want to sing the example using your song's lyrics, *also* sing it using numbers.

Ex. 1-9

In Ex. 1-10 you're given only the letter names. Let your mind supply both the numbers and the famous songs. Use numbers when you vocalize.

Ex. 1-10

In Ex. 1-11 you're on your own, but by now you should have no problem. Sing numbers.

Ex. 1-11

By the way, so far the three notes you've sung ("1," "3," and "5" in the key of C) have been written in only one octave—the octave starting on middle C. But what if you're a man with a low voice who can't sing high notes? Then you should mentally move the exercises down an octave (or to any octave—or even to any key—that's comfortable for your range). Because the relationship between the notes stays the same (and your thought process is the same) it makes no real difference, when learning to sight-sing, what octave or key you happen to be singing in (of course, it's a different matter if you're giving a performance and need to sing notes exactly as written).

Hearing "Low 5" and "High 1"

You've already learned the sound of "5" by thinking of the first note of "Deck the Halls." But that "5" happens to be five degrees *above* the tonic note (that is, it's G *above* middle C). What if you're sight-singing in the key of C and you see a G *below* middle C?

You can reckon that low G in one of two ways. One is to mentally move everything (your thought process, your scale, all your "famous songs") down an octave. Pretend that you don't like singing anything high, and you're going to think of your C scale as starting on C below middle C—and you're going to sing "Deck the Halls" in that lower range.

The other way, which I find more effective, is to extend the range of your C scale (that is, your one-octave scale ascending from middle C) by including extra notes beyond the one-octave range. I prefer this method because it's generally easier *not* to shift octaves mentally in the middle of a song. We'll call the fifth scale degree that appears *below* the tonic (G below middle C, in the key of C) "low 5." You can learn the sound of "low 5" by singing some famous songs that happen to begin on that degree. Below are the first two bars of three songs that happen to begin on "low 5."

Ex. 1-12

Sing them; hear how they all start on the same note—"low 5." My suggested song for remembering "low 5" is "Auld Lang Syne" ("Should auld acquaintance . . ."). Now choose "your song" (check out Appendix D for more possibilities).

Now here's the "special song" for "low 5." Sing upward, starting on a low note: "Five, one . . . Five, one . . . Five, one."

Ex. 1-13

"Five,   one"

You know the sound of "1" from the song "My Country, 'Tis of Thee." But what if you encounter, in the key of C, a high C (an octave above middle C). Again, you have two ways of reckoning this pitch. One way is to shift your entire thought process up an octave and pretend you're going to sing "My Country, 'Tis of Thee" in the higher octave. The better method—again, because shifting octaves in the middle of a songs is not easy—is to become aware of famous songs that begin on what we'll call "high 1." Note: Some people like to call this note "8"—either terminology is okay. Below are the beginnings of two famous songs that happen to begin on "high 1."

Ex. 1-14

See how they both start on the same note, high C ("high 1" in the key of C)? My suggested song for learning this degree is "Joy to the World." Now choose "your song" (see Appendix D).

Now here's the "special song" for "high 1." Sing downward, starting from a high note "One, five, three, one . . . One, five, three, one . . . One, five, three, one."

Ex. 1-15

"One,   five,   three,   one"

Exercises Using "Low 5" and "High 1"

The exercises that follow include your normal "1," "3," and "5" but add "low 5" and "high 1." Exs. 1-15 and 1-16 provide you with letter names, scale degrees, and syllables that correspond to my suggested songs. Use numbers to vocalize.

Ex. 1-16

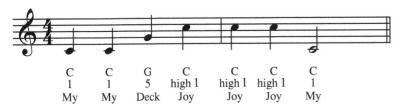

C	C	G	C	C	C	C
1	1	5	high 1	high 1	high 1	1
My	My	Deck	Joy	Joy	Joy	My

Ex. 1-17

C	G	C	E	E	E	G
1	low 5	1	3	3	3	5
My	Should	My	Way	Way	Way	Deck

Ex. 1-18 gives you only letter names and scale degrees.

Ex. 1-18

G	C	G	E	G	C	E
low 5	1	5	3	low 5	1	3

Ex. 1-19 gives you only letter names, but remember to vocalize using numbers.

Ex. 1-19

C	C	C	G	E	G	C

In Ex. 1-20 you're on your own again. As always, sing with numbers.

Ex. 1-20

A Word About Intervals

An *interval* is the distance between two notes, generally measured in scale degrees. For example, if C is scale degree 1 and E (above it) is scale degree 3, the two notes are said to be a 3rd apart. Similarly, the distance (or interval) from C up to G is a 5th (and you can count on your fingers to see that the distance is indeed five scale degrees: C–D–E–F–G). Special adjectives (*major, minor, perfect, augmented, diminished,* etc.) are sometimes placed before the numbers (as in *minor 3rd* or *diminished 5th*) to account for half step alterations between the notes in question (more on this in Appendix C).

Some people learn to sight-sing by memorizing not which famous songs begin on which scale degrees, but by looking at the first *two* notes of famous songs and determining what the interval between them is. They then memorize the sounds of all the ascending and descending intervals (about 24 different intervals). To sight-sing a particular note, they (1) look at it and determine is pitch, (2) look at the preceding note and determine *its* pitch, (3) determine what the interval is between the two notes, (4) remember the famous song whose first two notes correspond to that interval, and (5) sing the interval (from the previous note to the note in question).

Why is the interval system of sight-singing flawed? For one thing, it's harder (let's say twice as hard) to think of *two* notes (and the exact interval between them) than it is to think of just one note (as we do with our "scale degree" system). Another problem is that sometimes there *is* no previous note. Let's say, for example, you sing alto in a chorus, and your part enters in bar 9. How does your mind hear that first note if there's no other note before it to give you your "interval"? (When using scale degrees, of course, you don't need any "previous note.")

But there's still another, even more important, reason the interval method is flawed. When you learn the sound of an interval by listening to the first two notes of a famous song, your hear those notes, whether you realize it or not, within the context of the scale or key you're in. Let's say you know or learn that the sound of an ascending major 6th is the sound of the first two notes of "My Bonnie Lies over the Ocean." You decide that when you sight-sing you'll think of that song whenever you see two notes that constitute an ascending major 6th. But thinking of that song is effective only if the notes that make up the major 6th happen to have the same relationship to the scale that the first two notes of "My Bonnie" do; namely, the interval from the fifth scale degree up to the third degree (G up to E, in the key of C). Sticking with the key of C as an example, any other major 6th (D up to B, F up to D, or G up to E) sounds different—it doesn't sound like "My Bonnie." If you try to recall the sound of the first two notes of "My Bonnie" to sing one of those other major 6ths, either you won't be able to hear it in your mind, or you will hear it, but you'll inadvertently throw yourself into a new key.

So, then, is there no place for the interval technique in sight-singing? Sight-singing is a challenge, and, as with any challenge, you need an arsenal of tools or weapons in order to succeed. The scale degree technique should be your primary tool because it works effectively for about 95 percent of the music you'll encounter (it works for sight-singing what are known as *diatonic* tones; that is, the seven notes that exist within the key you're in—the white keys of a piano in the key of C, for example). But you need a bag of tricks to overcome that other five percent: passages that contain the five notes—known as *chromatic* tones—that *don't* exist in the key you're in (the black keys of a piano in the key of C, for example). Later on, when we begin to sight-sing chromatic tones, we'll talk about a number of techniques and mind tricks (yes, including intervals) that you can use to successfully sight-sing those chromatic tones.

CHAPTER 2:
SIGHT-SINGING SONGS WITH "1," "3," AND "5"

Crazy Christmas Carols

In Chapter 1 you used scale degrees "1," "3," and "5" to sing exercises, not songs. Now let's sing some songs. To get you started, I've devised something I call "Crazy Christmas Carols." They're famous carols, but they've been altered so that they use only three scale degrees (you guessed it, "1," "3," and "5")—but they generally follow the shape or contour (upward and downward motion) of the actual carols. Think of these crazy carols as a transition between singing exercises and singing your first real songs. Some of the notes will come to you automatically through your familiarity with the original carols; for other notes (the ones that have been altered), you'll need to depend on your familiarity with the sounds of the scale degrees. By the way, as you proceed, always work toward *memorizing* the sounds of the various scale degrees (as opposed to relying on the technique, discussed in Chapter 1, of pretending you're going to sing a famous song).

Notice that each crazy carol contains a box (a legend, or key) in the upper left corner that provides you with both the letter name and scale degree for each pitch used in the song. Such a box appears with every song you'll sight-sing throughout this book. Why, you might ask, do I provide a box when no such legends exist in real-life sight-singing situations. Well, you "theory nerds" out there automatically know which letter names correspond to which scale degrees in every key, and you don't need a legend. But for those of you who don't have a strong theory background (who don't already know these correlations), the box simply saves you the trouble of constantly having to turn to "Appendix B: Major and Minor Scales Identified by Letter Name and Scale Degree" at the back of the book. Note to non-theory people: Constantly work on memorizing the relationships between letter names and scale degrees in all keys!

In Ex. 2-1, "Crazy Jingle Bells," vocalize numbers (not letter names or famous song syllables), as always. Sing "Three, three, three; three, three, three; three, five, one, one, three," etc.

Ex. 2-1

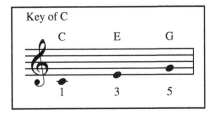

Ex. 2-2 is "Crazy Angels We Have Heard on High." Note that in the legend, the scale degree for "high 1" is in parentheses to distinguish it from regular "1."

Ex. 2-2

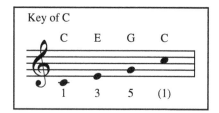

Bugle Calls

Now let's sing some real songs. The only problem is that, generally speaking, no real songs exist that use only "1," "3," and "5"—except bugle calls, that is. Since a bugle (unlike a trumpet) has no valves, it's capable of producing only the first, third, and fifth scale degrees! Now, some bugle calls (taps and reveille, for example) should already be familiar to you, so we won't use those to learn sight-signing. But Exs. 2-3 through 2-8 are actual bugle calls that are probably *unfamiliar* to you. All except the first of them contain both "5" and "low 5." Note: In the boxed legends, "low 5" is placed in parentheses to distinguish it from regular "5."

Ex. 2-3

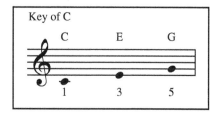

Ex. 2-4

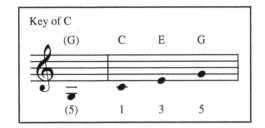

Ex. 2-5

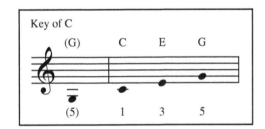

Ex. 2-6

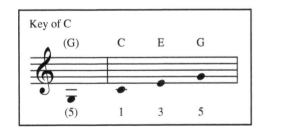

Ex. 2-7

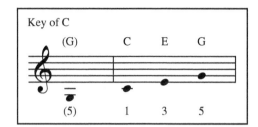

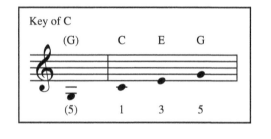

Ex. 2-8

CHAPTER 3:
LEARNING "2" AND "6"

Hearing "2" and "6"

Most famous songs happen to begin on the first, third, or fifth scale degree. That's why, if you look at Appendix D, you'll see that the number of titles presented for the other scale degrees ("2," "4," "6," and "7") is rather limited. If you're familiar with a famous song that begins on one of those degrees, you can use it as "your song." For example, for scale degree "2" you can use the Beatles' "Yesterday" (the first word of the lyric—"Yes-ter-day"—corresponds to scale degrees 2–1–1), or Barbra Streisand's "People" (the first word of the lyric—"Peo-ple"—corresponds to scale degrees 2–3). By the way, the technical term for the second scale degree is *supertonic*.

But because I want to present you with only *universally* familiar songs in teaching you the sounds of the various scale degrees, you'll need to modify your "trick" of pretending to sing the first note of a famous song. You may not be consciously aware of this, but just as your musical mind can "pull from the air" the first note of any familiar song, it can do likewise with notes that occur *within a song*. Let's give it a try. See if you can hear just the last two notes of "The Star Spangled Banner." Here's what they look like:

Ex. 3-1

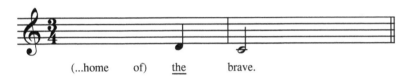

(...home   of)   the   brave.

Now try to hear just the last two notes of "The Twelve Days of Christmas." They look like this:

Ex. 3-2

...and a partridge in a pear tree.

Do you see that each of those next-to-last notes is a D (scale degree "2" in the key of C)? If you can hear that first note (D) of the final two-note phrase, then you can hear scale degree "2."

My suggested syllable for "2" is "pear" (from the last two notes of "The Twelve Days of Christmas"). Now choose "your song." It can be one that actually does begin on "2" ("Yesterday," for example), or one containing an inner phrase that begins on "2."

Now here's the "special song" for "2." Sing "Two, one . . . Two, one . . . Two, one."

Ex. 3-3

"Two,   one"

Now let's tackle "6," whose technical name is *submediant.* We'll look at both the regular "6" (that is, "6" above the tonic) and what we'll call "low 6."

The first note of Stephen Foster's "Jeanie with the Light Brown Hair" demonstrates the sound of "6."

Ex. 3-4

I   dream   of Jean - ie with the   light   brown▁ hair...

My suggested syllable for "6" is "I" (as in "I dream of Jean-ie"). Now choose your song and syllable (remember to check out Appendix D).

For "low 6," let's use an inner phrase of "Old MacDonald Had a Farm."

Ex. 3-5

(Old   MacDonald)   had   a   farm.   E - I - E - I - O...

For "low 6" you can use the syllable "had" (as in "had a farm"), or you can stick with the same song and syllable you chose for "regular 6," but mentally transpose "your song" down an octave.

Now here are "special songs" for "6" and "low 6."

Ex. 3-6

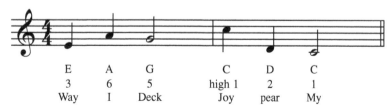

"Six,   five,   three,   one"   "Six,   seven,   one"

Exercises Using "2" and "6"

In Exs. 3-7 and 3-8, you're given letter names, scale degrees, and my suggested syllables. Sing numbers.

Ex. 3-7

E	A	G	C	D	C
3	6	5	high 1	2	1
Way	I	Deck	Joy	pear	My

Ex. 3-8

C	A	E		G	C	D
1	low 6	3		5	high 1	2
My	had	Way		Deck	Joy	pear

In Ex. 3-9 you're given only scale degrees and letter names. Ex. 3-10 provides just letter names, and in Ex. 3-11 you're on your own. As always, sing numbers.

Ex. 3-9

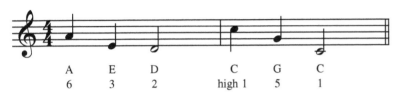

A	E	D		C	G	C
6	3	2		high 1	5	1

Ex. 3-10

C	C	A		E	G	D

Ex. 3-11

CHAPTER 4:
SIGHT-SINGING SONGS WITH "1," "2," "3," "5," AND "6"

Now let's sing some songs using all the scale degrees you've learned so far—"1," "2," "3," "5," and "6." As mentioned in the Introduction, these are actual songs, not contrived exercises. We'll start out in the key of C, then sing in a couple of "sharp" keys (keys with sharps in their signatures) and a couple of "flat" keys (keys with flats in their signatures).

Exs. 4-1 and 4-2 are both in the key of C. Each uses "high 1" as well as regular "1."

Before you sing these two examples, let's add something to your bag of tricks. You, like anyone else who listens to Western (non-Asian) music, is familiar with the sound of the ascending or descending major scale. If, when you sight-sing, you see a series of two or more notes that occur consecutively in the major scale, you can determine the sound of just the first of those notes, then simply sing up or down the scale for the rest of them (rather than reckon each individually). For example, in Ex. 4-1, you can determine (using the "scale degree" technique you've learned) the sound of the E that occurs on beat 3 of measure 8, then simply sing down the major scale for the following D and C. You can use the "singing up or down the major scale" technique for any consecutive scale degrees you encounter throughout the rest of this book.

Ex. 4-1

Ex. 4-2

Ex. 4-3 is in the key of G and is your first example in a key other than C. Because in the key of G the G note is the tonic, think of your song (or syllable or sound) for "1" whenever you see a G (not when you see a C, as you did when you were in the key of C). Likewise, think "2" for A, "3" for B, "5" for D, and "6" for E. Refer to the boxed legend for these number-letter relationships, if necessary. The song uses both regular and high "1."

Ex. 4-3

Ex. 4-4 is in the key of D. If necessary, use the boxed legend to see the number-letter relationships in that key (that is, D is "1," E is "2," and so on). Notice that this song extends above "high 1." The E's ("2") and F-sharps ("3") that occur in bars 11 and 12 are in the next higher octave. To sing them, mentally transpose your thought process (your songs, syllables, or "special songs" that you like to use for "2" and "3") up an octave. For example, if you still think of the syllable "way" (as in "Way down upon the Swanee River") for "3," pretend you're going to sing "Swanee River" in a higher than usual octave.

By the way, this example illustrates the reason I like to call the high tonic note "high 1" or "(1)" instead of "8": the high tonic often *becomes* the regular tonic, "1," in the new (higher) octave. Note that the reason the high "2" and high "3" are not shown in parentheses in the legend is that they are thought of not as upper extensions to your normal range, but as the *actual* "2" and "3" of your new, higher range.

Ex. 4-4

Ex. 4-5 is your first song in a "flat" key. In the key of F, the F note is "1." Use the legend, if necessary, to see how other pitches in the key of F translate into scale degrees. This song uses "low 5," "low 6," and "high 1." You should think of those pitches as extensions of your regular one-octave range (not as notes in other octaves). Note that pitches that appear below the low tonic are shown in parentheses in the legend.

Ex. 4-5

Ex. 4-6 is in the key of E-flat. Again, use the legend, if necessary, to translate letter names into scale degrees. Again, think of "low 5," "low 6," and "high 1" as extensions of your normal one-octave range.

Ex. 4-6

CHAPTER 5:
LEARNING "4" AND "7"

Hearing "4" and "7"

Scale degrees "4" and "7" are presented last because they are probably the most difficult to hear. Why? Because each, being a half step away from a member of the tonic triad, clashes with the tonic triad (in the key of C, for example, F clashes with E and B clashes with C).

Not many famous songs begin on the fourth scale degree, whose technical name is *subdominant.* On exception is Donovan's 1968 hit "Jennifer Juniper." If you're familiar with it, you might use it as "your song" for "4." But if we include as possibilities songs whose inner or closing phrases begin on "4," then we have more choice. My suggestion for "4" is the second phrase of "Twinkle, Twinkle, Little Star."

Ex. 5-1

(Twin - kle, twin - kle, lit - tle star;) how   I   won - der   where   you   are.

Ex. 5-2

"Four   three   one"

Scale degree "7," whose technical name is *leading tone* or *subtonic,* is also not a common starting note for famous songs. If you know "Don't Let the Sun Catch You Cryin'" (a 1964 hit by Gerry and the Pacemakers), you can use that as "your song." My suggestion for "7" is the next-to-last note of the second phrase of "Joy to the World." Here I'm asking you to hear (to "pull out of the air," so to speak) not the first note of a song or the first note of an inner phrase of a song, but a *single isolated note* within a song. Can you do it?

Ex. 5-3

Let   earth   receive   her   King.

Here are two more songs ("America, the Beautiful" and "Sing a Song of Sixpence") that contain a conspicuous seventh scale degree within an interior phrase. Either of these can serve as "your song" (or "syllable") for "7."

Ex. 5-4

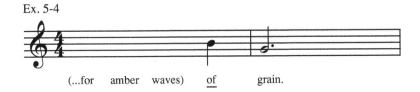

(...for   amber   waves)   of   grain.

Ex. 5-5

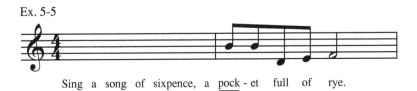

Sing a song of sixpence, a pock - et full of rye.

In the examples above, "7" occurs above "1." If "7" happens to fall a half step below "1," you can think of it as "low 7" (that is, think of it as a lower extension of your normal one-octave range rather than as a "normal 7" in a new, lower octave. One song whose first note perfectly demonstrates the sound of "low 7" is "Danny Boy.

Ex. 5-6

Oh,   Dan - ny   boy...

Here are your "special songs" for "7" and "low 7." Remember that you should play all your "special songs" on an instrument until you have them memorized. As mentioned earlier, you can actually use a "special song" *instead* of a famous song to learn the sound of any scale degree.

Ex. 5-7

"Seven   one"   "Seven   one"

Exercises Using "4" and "7"

Each of the following exercises contains all seven scale degrees (here in the key of C). The first two provide you with my suggested syllables (in addition to letter names and scale degrees). Note that I've indicated "how" (as in "how I wonder where you are") for "4" and "her" (as in "her King") for "7" (but you can, as always, substitute "your syllables"). The third example provides only letter names and scale degrees, and the fourth provides only letter names. The last provides musical notation only.

Because you sing numbers (instead of letter names or "do-re-mi") when you sight-sing, you might wonder how to vocalize "7"; that is, you see only a single note, but your vocalization would seem to require *two* syllables ("sev-en"). The answer is that, for the purpose of learning to sight-sing, it's okay for you to sing both syllables ("sev-en") even though you see just one note. The "sight-singing police" won't rush in and arrest you. (If, on the other hand, your sensibilities simply won't allow you to sing two syllables on one note, try singing "sev.")

Ex. 5-8

A	F	B	G	C	D	E
6	4	7	5	1	2	3
I	how	her	Deck	My	pear	Way

Ex. 5-9

E	C	D	B	F	A	G
3	1	2	7	4	6	5
Way	My	pear	her	how	I	Deck

Ex. 5-10

A   E   C   F   D   G   B
6   3   1   4   2   5   7

Ex. 5-11

E   G   A   D   B   C   F

Ex. 5-12

CHAPTER 6:
SIGHT-SINGING SONGS WITH ALL SEVEN SCALE DEGREES

In this chapter you'll sight-sing eight songs in various keys. The first four add scale degree "4" to the other degrees ("1," "2," "3," " 5," and "6") you've already worked with. If you're singing in a key that you're not accustomed to, remember that you can use that song's boxed legend to find the key's number-letter relationships. As usual, lower and higher extensions ("low 5" and "high 1," for example) to your normal one-octave range are shown in parentheses in the legends.

Ex. 6-1

Ex. 6-2

Ex. 6-3

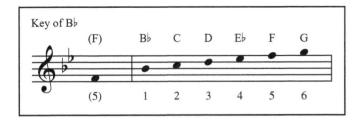

Ex. 6-4

The next four songs include all seven scale degrees. Because this is your first time singing actual songs using all seven scale degrees, I've made things easy for you by choosing melodies that have only a one-octave range, extending from scale degree "1" up to scale degree "high 1"; that is, they contain no lower extensions and no upper extensions above "high 1."

Ex. 6-5

Ex. 6-6

Ex. 6-7

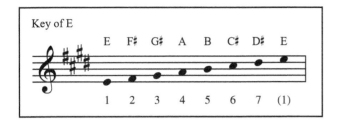

Ex. 6-8

CHAPTER 7: NAME THAT TUNE

You've completed half the chapters of the book, and most of the hard work has already been accomplished. Now let's have some fun with a game called "Name That Tune." In this chapter you're given the beginnings of 21 very famous songs (in various keys), and it's up to you to discover what they are (don't peek at Appendix E yet) by using your knowledge of the sounds of the various scale degrees.

By the way, don't think of this chapter as purely "fun and games." Sometimes sight-singing works "silently"; that is, instead of actually singing aloud, someone (a conductor, music editor, music publisher, etc.) might look at a melody and hear it only in his mind. You need to be proficient in both "out loud" and "silent" sight-singing. By identifying famous songs merely by looking at their pitches, you demonstrate that you can sight-sing "silently" (or, to put it another way, you can hear written music in your head).

I haven't indicated the durations of the notes in this chapter (because sometimes a song can be identified by its melodic rhythm alone), but I have placed bar lines between groups of notes to give you a bit of help.

Ex. 7-1

Ex. 7-2

Ex. 7-3

Ex. 7-4

Ex. 7-5

Ex.7-6

Ex. 7-7

Ex. 7-8

Ex. 7-9

Ex. 7-10

Ex. 7-11

Ex. 7-12

Ex. 7-13

Ex. 7-14

Ex. 7-15

Ex. 7-16

Ex. 7-17

Ex. 7-18

Ex. 7-19

Ex. 7-20

Ex. 7-21

CHAPTER 8:
SONGS FOR PRACTICE (ALL PITCHES, ALL KEYS)

I like to think of this chapter as the "heart" of the book. Here is where you really sight-sing with no restrictions, using everything you've learned. You'll be singing songs in all major keys (up to four sharps or flats in the key signature), you'll be using all seven scale degrees, and you'll be encountering upper and lower extensions to your normal one-octave range. Sometimes you'll even need or want to "shift octaves" in your mind. You won't learn anything new in this chapter; these songs are for practice, practice, practice.

The 22 songs contained here run through the various major keys, starting in C, and then adding sharps and flats, alternately, one at a time, to the signature. We have four songs in the key of C, then three each in G and F, and then two each in D, B-flat, A, E-flat, E, and A-flat. Within each key the songs are presented in order of increasing difficulty (based on such criteria as extent of range, number of upper and lower extensions, number of measures, etc.).

Ex. 8-1

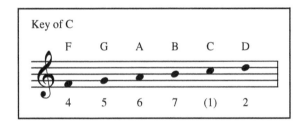

Ex. 8-2

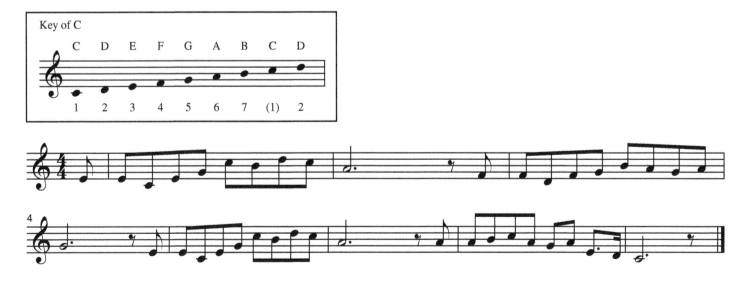

Ex. 8-3

Ex. 8-4

Ex. 8-5

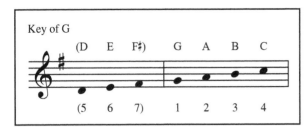

Ex. 8-6

Ex. 8-7

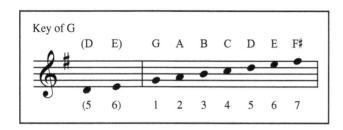

Ex. 8-8

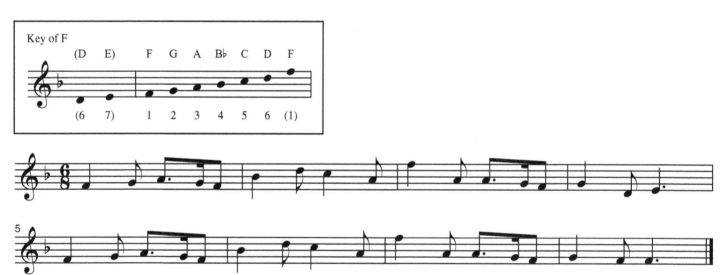

Ex. 8-9

Ex. 8-11

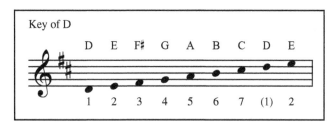

Ex. 8-12

Ex. 8-13

Ex. 8-15

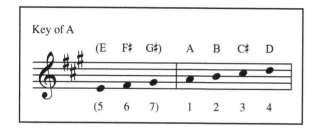

Ex. 8-16

Ex. 8-17

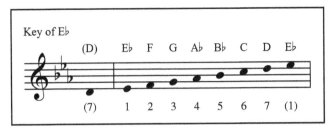

Ex. 8-18

Ex. 8-19

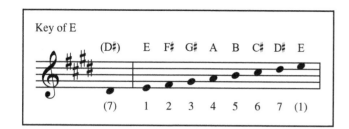

Ex. 8-20

Ex. 8-21

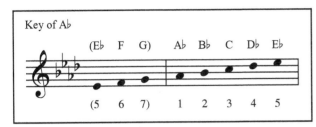

Ex. 8-22

CHAPTER 9:
MINOR KEYS

The "scale degree" system of sight-singing works beautifully for diatonic songs in major keys; in fact, it works so well that knowing how to use it is tantamount to having perfect pitch (once the key has been established). But how well does it work for sight-singing songs in minor keys or songs containing chromatic tones (notes out of the key)? The answer is that the system can still work for you, though probably not quite as effortlessly. This chapter and the next cover sight-singing in minor keys, and the following two chapters discuss how to sight-sing chromatic tones.

Understanding Minor Scales

Before we tackle learning the sounds of the various degrees of the minor scale, let's review how minor scales are constructed. The topic is thorny because, unlike the major scale, the minor scale exists in three different forms—the *natural minor*, the *melodic minor*, and the *harmonic minor*. Furthermore, not everyone refers to the degrees of the minor scale in the same way. So, depending on who's talking and which form of the minor scale they're referring to (and which other scale they're comparing it to), you might hear such seemingly confusing phrases as "flat-6," "6," "sharp-6," and "raised 6," all to refer to the sixth scale degree in minor!

To get a handle on all this, let's start by taking a look at the C major scale.

Ex. 9-1

Now, if you take the sixth degree of C major (A) and use it to begin a new scale (but use the pitches of the C major scale), you get A, B, C, D, E, F, G—otherwise known as the *A natural minor scale*. This minor scale occurs "naturally" by beginning on "6" of the "parent" major scale. In Ex. 9-2 two rows of scale degree numbers are indicated below the notes. The top row shows the scale degrees of the A natural minor scale unto itself; the bottom row shows scale degrees *as compared to the C major scale* (that is, while the first note, A, is "1" of A minor, it is "6" of C major).

Ex. 9-2

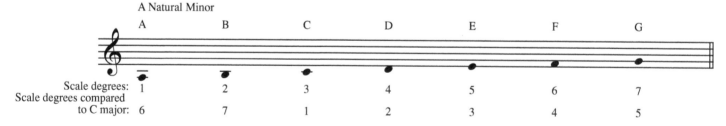

By the way, a major and minor scale that share the same pitches and key signature are said to be *related* to each other. That is, A minor is the *relative minor* of C major; conversely, C major is the *relative major* of A minor. Of course, this principle applies not only to C major (and its relative, A minor), but to all keys. For example, E minor is the relative minor of G major (each has a key signature of one sharp), and E-flat major is the relative major of C minor (each has a key signature of three flats).

Now—because we still want to stick with C (even in its minor form) as "square one" for theoretical study—take a look at the C natural minor scale and see how it relates not to its relative major scale (E-flat major) but to what is known as its *parallel* major scale—that is, the major scale that begins on the same note (in this case C). In Ex. 9-3 you again see two rows of scale degrees. The top row shows the scale degrees of the C natural minor scale unto itself; the bottom row shows scale degrees compared to the parallel major—C major. You can see that, depending on which scale is being used for comparison or analysis, one person might refer to A-flat as "6" while someone else might call it "flat-6." But either way, they're talking about A-flat.

Ex. 9-3

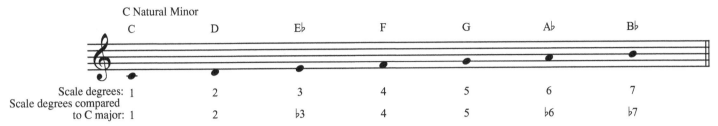

	C	D	Eb	F	G	Ab	Bb
Scale degrees:	1	2	3	4	5	6	7
Scale degrees compared to C major:	1	2	b3	4	5	b6	b7

Ex. 9-4 shows what is known as the *C melodic minor scale*. Compared to the natural minor scale, this scale uses a raised "6" (A-natural) and raised "7" (B-natural) in its ascending form; but in its descending form it is identical to the natural minor scale (that is, it uses B-flat and A-flat). Three rows of scale degrees are given here so that you can see how the scale degrees relate to the C melodic minor scale itself (top row), the parallel major scale, C major (middle row), and the parallel natural minor scale (bottom row).

Ex. 9-4

C Melodic Minor

	C	D	Eb	F	G	A♮	B♮	C	Bb	Ab	G	F	Eb	D	C
Scale degrees:	1	2	3	4	5	6	7	6	7	(1)	7	6	5	4	3
Scale degrees compared to C major:	1	2	b3	4	5	6	7	(1)	b7	b6	5	4	b3	2	1
Scale degrees compared to C natural minor:	1	2	3	4	5	#6	#7	(1)	7	6	5	4	3	2	1

Ex. 9-5 shows what is known as the *C harmonic minor scale*. Compared to the parallel major, it uses a lowered "3" (E-flat) and a lowered "6" (A-flat). Compared to the parallel natural minor it uses a raised "7" (B-natural). As such, people often say that this scale uses "flat-6 and sharp-7," even though the comparisons of the two degrees in question are to two different parallel scales.

Ex. 9-5

C Harmonic Minor

	C	D	Eb	F	G	Ab	B♮
Scale degrees:	1	2	3	4	5	6	7
Scale degrees compared to C major:	1	2	b3	4	5	b6	7
Scale degrees compared to C natural minor:	1	2	3	4	5	6	#7

Hearing Scale Degrees in Minor Keys

Now that you understand how minor scales are constructed and how their scale degrees are named, let's learn the sounds of the minor key scale degrees. I'll be giving you three different methods for learning these sounds; I call them the "altering the major scale" method, the "special songs in minor" method, and the "famous song" method. As you become familiar with these methods, you'll choose the one that works best for you (but as you'll see, I'll be recommending that you use the "special songs in minor" method).

"Altering the Major Scale" Method

In looking at the examples above, you probably noticed that when you compare any minor scale to its parallel major scale, the first, second, fourth, and fifth scale degrees are identical (for example, both C major and C minor contain the notes C, D, F, and G). Only scale degrees "3," "6," and "7" differ between major and minor (and in the ascending melodic minor scale, only "3" differs). So you might decide that when you sight-sing in C minor, you'll use your knowledge of the sounds of "1," "2," "4," and "5" (as learned for the major scale) to reckon C, D, F, and G. (Of course, we're using the key of C minor here only as an example; the principle applies to all keys.) Then, for "3," "6," and "7" (or—to use the terminology we employ when comparing minor to parallel major— "flat-3," "flat-6," and "flat-7") you can think of the third, sixth, and seventh degrees of the major scale, but in your mind lower them a half step—assuming you can hear the interval of a half step, that is (for a discussion of half steps, see Chapter 11). But even if this "altering the major scale" method allows you to produce pitches correctly when you sight-sing in minor, I don't recommend it (except as a tool in your "bag of tricks") because, after all, you'll be thinking in the "wrong" key.

"Special Songs in Minor" Method

When you learned the sounds of the various scale degrees in the major scale, you used the "first note of a famous song" as your principle method and "special songs" as a backup method (if you don't remember what "special songs" are, review Chapter 1). For minor scale degrees, I recommend the reverse. Why? Because not very many universally famous songs in minor keys exist whose first notes are immediately recognizable to everyone as particular scale degrees.

Ex. 9-6 shows the "special songs" for each scale degree in minor. By the way, in this section and the next (where I discuss the "famous song" method), I'm showing the sixth and seventh scale degrees in their natural (lowered compared to parallel major) form only. Why? Because the raised versions of "6" and "7" (A-natural and B-natural in the key of C minor) have a "major" sound, and you can use your knowledge of those sounds—that is, the sound of "6" and "7" of the major scale, as learned in Chapters 3 and 5—even when you sight-sing in minor keys. Play each of these minor key "special songs" over and over. Then sing them over and over until they're memorized. When you sight-sing in a minor key, think of the "special song" that corresponds to the note you want to sing—then sing that "special song's" first note. With practice, you won't really need to think of the "special song"; the scale degree will have become memorized.

Ex. 9-6

"1"
"One"

"2"
"Two,   one"

"3"
"Three,   one"

"4"
"Four,   three,   one"

"5"
"Five,   three,   one"

"6"
"Six,   five,   three,   one"

"7"   "low 7"
"Seven,   one"   "Seven,   one"

"Famous Song" Method

You'll remember that in Chapter 3 you were sometimes asked to hear in your mind not the first note of a famous song, but a note in the middle of a song (sometimes the first note of a phrase, sometimes an interior note of a phrase). You thought of the word "pear" ("partridge in a *pear* tree") to learn the sound of "2." If you were able to do that in a major key, you can employ the same technique in minor to learn all seven scale degrees from just one famous song!

Ex. 9-7 shows the beginning of "God Rest Ye Merry, Gentlemen" in C minor with certain notes identified by (minor key) scale degree. For example, the first syllable, "God," is "1" and the third syllable, "ye," is "5." Each designated note can be thought of as the beginning of a "phrase" within the song. Each of these phrases is "your famous song (phrase)" for learning the scale degree in question—just as in Chapter 5 you used the phrase "how I wonder where you are" to learn the sound of "4" (in major). Practice singing these phrases until the sounds of the scale degrees become memorized.

Ex. 9-7

When you first started out sight-singing in major keys, you thought of syllables that corresponded to famous songs—"your songs." Using those syllables as lyrics to the C major scale, we get:

Ex. 9-8

Let's do the same thing for the minor scale using your syllables from "God Rest Ye." Including "low 7," and indicating both scale degree numbers and "God Rest Ye" syllables, we get:

Ex. 9 - 9

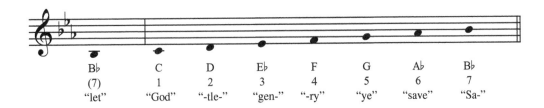

Exercises Using Scale Degrees in Minor Keys

Using any of the techniques described above, sight-sing the following exercises (all in the key of C minor and all using the seven scale degrees of the C natural minor scale). Exs. 9-10 and 9-11 provide you with letter names, scale degrees, and "God Rest Ye" syllables (in case you choose to use that method). Ex. 9-12 gives you only letter names and scale degrees, and Ex. 9-13 gives you only letter names. For Ex. 9-14 you're on your own.

Ex. 9-10

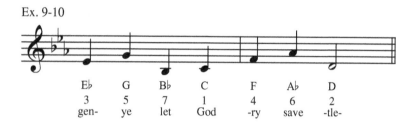

Ex. 9-11

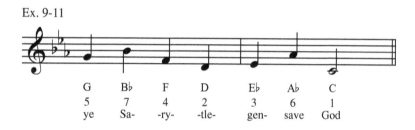

Ex. 9-12

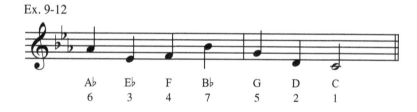

Ex. 9-13

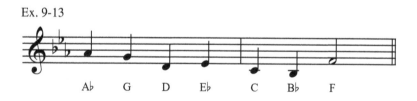

Ex. 9-14

Note: It might occur to you that since the examples on this page use a key signature of three flats and contain no accidentals, you could avoid thinking in minor by pretending that you're in the key of E-flat major—the relative major (and singing Ex. 9-10, for example, using major scale degrees "1," "3," "low 5," "low 6," "2," "4," "low 7"). While this trick actually works, I don't recommend it, except for an emergency. Why? For one thing, you'd be thinking in the wrong key. For another, it's ineffective for minor melodies that contain altered tones; that is, raised sixth and seventh degrees, as in the melodic or harmonic forms of the minor scale (you'd be thinking in E-flat major and contending with A-naturals and B-naturals!).

CHAPTER 10:
SIGHT-SINGING SONGS IN MINOR KEYS

In this chapter you'll sight-sing ten songs in various minor keys. Note that if you are familiar enough with the sound of the minor scale, you can sing phrases of consecutive scale degrees by determining the sound of only the first note of the phrase; the others will flow automatically up or down the scale. Also note that, compared to its parallel major scale, while the minor scale always contains a lowered third degree, its sixth and seventh degrees are sometimes lowered and sometimes not (depending on the form of the minor scale used).

Here are some points of interest about the songs in this chapter:

- Ex. 10-1 contains no "6"; "7" is from natural minor scale.

- Ex. 10-2 also contains no "6"; its "7" (also natural minor) is low (below the tonic).

- Exs. 10-3 and 10-4 contain no "6"; their "7"'s, both low, are from the harmonic minor scale (that is, they are raised compared to the parallel natural minor scale).

- Ex. 10-5 uses the natural minor scale; "7" and "1" occur in both the high and low positions; "6" is approached stepwise.

- Ex. 10-6 also uses the natural minor scale; "6" is approached by a skip from above; "5," "1," "2," and "3" occur in both low and high octaves.

- Exs. 10-7 and 10-8 both use the harmonic minor scale; that is, they use the unraised "6" but the raised "7" (compared to the parallel natural minor scale).

- Ex. 10-9 uses the melodic minor scale (ascending form) in its lower register; that is, it has a raised "6" and raised "7" (compared to the natural minor scale). However, at the top of its range it uses an unraised "7."

- Ex. 10-10 uses a mixed minor scale—a combination or harmonic minor and natural minor; that is, it has unraised "6," but it uses both an unraised and raised "7" (in the same register).

Ex. 10-1

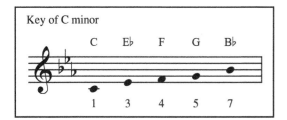

Ex. 10-2

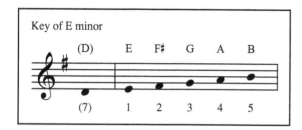

Ex. 10-3

Ex. 10-4

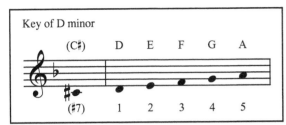

Ex. 10-5

Ex. 10-6

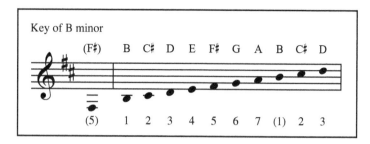

Ex. 10-7

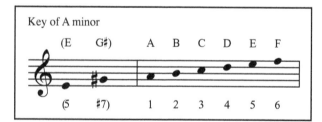

Ex. 10-8

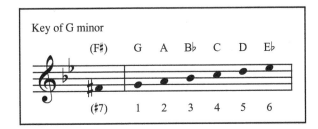

Ex. 10-9

Ex. 10-10

CHAPTER 11:
CHROMATIC TONES

The seven notes that make up a particular major or minor scale are known as *diatonic* notes, and the notes outside the scale (or key) are known as *chromatic* tones. For example, in the key of C major, the diatonic notes are the white keys of the piano keyboard and the chromatic tones are the black keys. Because the piano keyboard makes it so easy to visually or mentally separate the diatonic from the chromatic in the key of C major, we'll stick with that key for the theoretical discussions and music examples that follow in this chapter. Once you understand the principles presented here, you can apply them to any key—and you can practice sight-singing chromatic melodies in various keys in the next chapter.

The scale degree system of sight-singing allows you to easily hear in your mind all seven diatonic tones. How can you hear the other five tones—the chromatic ones? I'm not going to ask you to memorize a famous song or "special song" that happens to begin on each of these out-of-the-key notes (hardly any such songs exist). But there are several tricks you can use, and each is discussed below. Make sure to add each trick to your personal "bag of tricks" as we go along.

Attaching a Chromatic Note to Its Neighbor
In Ex. 11-1 you can see that the chromatic tone D-sharp occurs between two E's. A note that moves stepwise away from, then back to, another note is called a *neighboring tone*. Here the D-sharp is a *chromatic* lower neighbor to E. (Note that if a D-natural were in this position, it would be called a *diatonic* lower neighbor.)

Ex. 11-1

You can hear the sound of D-sharp in your mind if you know two things: the sound of E ("3") and the sound of the interval of a half step. The trick is to "attach" the D-sharp to the E; that is, think of E (but don't sing it), then think of E's chromatic lower neighbor (which is a half step below). But before we apply that trick, let's review half steps.

A *half step* is a musical interval; it's the distance between any two consecutive notes on a piano keyboard (the distance between C and C-sharp, or between D and E-flat, or between E and F, for example). By the way, half steps that share a letter name (C and C-sharp, for example) are known as *chromatic half steps* (they can never occur within the same major or minor scale); half steps with consecutive letter names (E and F, for example) are called *diatonic half steps* (they can exist within the same scale). The *chromatic scale* is an ascending or descending scale (starting on any note) made up of all 12 consecutive tones (including all white and black keys) of the piano keyboard.

You're probably already familiar with the sound of the chromatic scale and of the half step, but if not (or for review) go to the keyboard (or your instrument) and, starting on any note, play the chromatic scale upward and downward. Sing it up and then down (over and over, if necessary), until it's memorized. Next, play just two consecutive notes from the scale; play them upward, then downward. Try singing this interval. Now memorize the sound of the interval (that is, memorize the sound of both an ascending and descending half step).

Now try singing Ex. 11-1. Hear the E in your mind, then hear its chromatic lower neighbor and sing it. When you vocalize, since you're using numerals, sing "One, three, sharp-two, three" (and don't worry that you're actually singing two syllables—"sharp-two"—on one note).

In case you're having trouble hearing the lower chromatic half step, I'll give you a crutch—but just this once. Ex. 11-2 is the beginning of the famous Christmas carol "O Little Town of Bethlehem." It contains the same chromatic lower neighbor as the one in Ex. 11-1. Both the actual song lyrics and your vocalization syllables appear beneath the notes.

Ex. 11-2

O   lit - tle   town   of...
"Three three   three sharp-two three"

Note that when you hear or sing the D-sharp in Ex. 11-1 or Ex. 11-2, you relate the note not to the tonic, C (as you did when singing diatonic scale degrees), but to its neighbor, E.

In Ex. 11-3 you attach the chromatic tone (F-sharp) to *its* neighbor, G. Sing "Three, five, sharp-four, five."

Ex. 11-3

Ex. 11-4 uses an *upper* chromatic neighbor. Attach the A-flat to G. After hearing the sound of G ("5") in your mind, think of the sound of an *ascending* half step. Sing "Five, five, flat-six, five."

Ex. 11-4

Using the Chromatic Scale to Hear Chromatic Passing Tones

Sometimes a chromatic note is placed between two consecutive scale degrees. For example (still in the key of C), you might see the ascending phrase "D–D-sharp–E" or the descending phrase "A–A-flat–G"; those out-of-key notes are known as *chromatic passing tones* (they "pass" between diatonic scale degrees). (By the way, a *diatonic passing tone*—which we're not concerned with here—is a scale degree that's not a member of the chord being played and that passes between two other scale degrees a 3rd apart; for example, if a C major chord is being played and the melody moves from C to D to E, the D is a diatonic passing tone.)

Exs. 11-5, 11-6, and 11-7 each contain an ascending chromatic passing tone, and Exs. 11-8 and 11-9 each contain a descending chromatic passing tone. To hear and sing these tones, you can employ one of two techniques. You can either "attach" the chromatic note to an adjacent diatonic tone, as you did before, or, better, you can see that the three-note chromatic phrase (D–D-sharp–E in Ex. 11-5, for example) is part of the chromatic scale (whose sound you already know). Simply hear and sing the first note of the phrase (which happens to be a diatonic scale degree whose sound you know), then sing up or down the chromatic scale until you come to the next normal (diatonic) degree. Now sight-sing the five examples below.

Ex. 11-5

Ex. 11-6

Ex. 11-7

Ex. 11-8

Ex. 11-9

Borrowing from Minor

Sometimes when you sight-sing in a major key you see chromatic tones that aren't half-step neighbors or passing tones. If the chromatic notes happen to be flat-3, flat-6, or flat-7 (that is, if in the key of C you see passages containing E-flat, A-flat, or B-flat) you can hear those tones by employing a trick called "borrowing from minor." In Chapter 9 you learned how to hear the scale degrees of the natural minor scale. To sight-sing Exs. 11-10 and 11-11 below, when you get to measure 2, simply *pretend* you're in the key of C minor (instead of C major), and you should have no trouble reckoning the chromatic tones.

Ex. 11-10

Ex. 11-11

Changing the Tonic

Sometimes a song begins in one key but, as it progresses, moves into another key, or key area, without an actual key signature change. For example, the melody below (Ex. 11-12) is the beginning of "O Come, All Ye Faithful." It begins in C but cadences (ends) in G (without a change of key signature); that is, the final G sounds like "1," not "5."

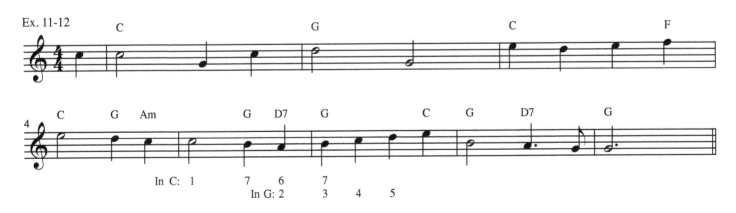

If you were unfamiliar with this song and didn't see (or hear) the background harmony (chords) you might not know that the final G sounds like "1." You might sing the entire melody in the key of C (hearing the final G as "5"). But if someone were accompanying you by playing chords, you'd need to employ a mind trick known as "changing the tonic" when you got to measure 5 or 6. Why? Because it's difficult or impossible to continue to think in C when someone is playing background chords (G–C–D7–G) in the key of G. In the example, I've shown scale degree numbers in both keys where the transition from C to G takes place. Start out by thinking in the key of C, but in the middle of the song *shift your thinking* so that G becomes "1," not "5"—think in G!

The next melody (Ex. 11-13) is the beginning of "Pomp and Circumstance" (you know, that song they play at high school and college graduation ceremonies); it also starts in C but cadences in G.

Ex. 11-13

In C: 3   #4 5
   In G: 7 1   2   5

Assume for the moment that you were unfamiliar with this song and needed a technique or trick for reckoning the F-sharp in measure 10. You could "attach" it, as before, to the G (but you don't want to do that because the chord progression tells you that you're about to move out of the key of C). By changing the tonic in your mind (from C major to G major), you convert a chromatic tone ("sharp-4" in the key of C) to a diatonic one ("7" in the key of G) whose sound you already know! Again, in the example, I've indicated scale degrees in both keys where the transition takes place.

Whenever you see a passage in one key that contains a set of accidentals that seem to belong to another key—whether the song actually modulates (changes keys) or not—you can use the trick of *pretending* that you're in that other key. For example, if you're sight-singing in the key of C and suddenly all the B's have flats in front of them, try thinking in the key of F (whose signature contains one flat—B-flat). Let F become "1" in your mind. By "changing the tonic" you convert chromatic tones (of the original key) into diatonic tones (of the new key).

Using Intervals

In Ex. 11-14 below, it appears that the melody has been created simply by outlining the background chords. If you were to sight-sing that phrase, how could you hear the G-sharp in measure 2? After all, you can't "attach" it to a neighbor, and it's not a passing tone. You might pretend that bar 2 isn't in the key of C, but is instead in the key of A or E—and that may or may not be a good idea, depending on what might come next.

Ex.11-14

For cases like this, which involve chromatic tones that are skipped into and out of, it's useful to know the sounds of the various intervals. Although in general I strongly oppose the use of intervals in sight-singing (check out the last section of Chapter 1 for my reasons), sometimes they are indeed the best (or only) choice. In this example we have an E moving up to G-sharp—the interval of a major 3rd. You already know the sound of E; if you knew the sound of an ascending major 3rd, you could find G-sharp.

In Appendix C, I explain interval terminology and I show the two notes (using C as the lower) that make up each of the 12 ascending and descending intervals. But for the reasons explained at the end of Chapter 1, I don't give you any famous songs for learning the sounds of the intervals. Try to memorize their sounds simply by playing the intervals over and over on your instrument. Sing each interval. Next, transpose them so that notes other than C are on the bottom. By the way, Appendix C also includes a chart that shows some strangely named intervals and indicates which common intervals they sound the same as.

Mixing It Up
Your sight-singing "bag of tricks" now contains a number of effective "tools." While it's sometimes obvious which tool or trick you should use in a particular situation, sometimes it isn't immediately clear. Take, for example, Ex. 11-15:

Ex.11-15

How should you reckon that F-sharp? You could "attach" it to G as a chromatic lower neighbor. You could use your knowledge of intervals and sing it as a whole step (major 2nd) above E. Or you could, perhaps starting at the E, pretend you were in the key of G (and think of it as "7" in the new key). The point is, you can use any (or all) of those tricks; it's up to you.

In the next chapter you'll sight-sing songs containing chromatic tones is various keys. I'll suggest tricks for sight-singing those tones, but you're free to use whichever technique works best for you.

CHAPTER 12:
SIGHT-SINGING SONGS WITH CHROMATIC TONES

The 13 songs in this chapter are in various keys; they all contain chromatic tones. When sight-singing them, vocalize, as always, using numerals. For altered tones (chromatic notes), add the prefix "sharp" or "flat" before the number; for example, for B-natural in the key of F sing "sharp-four," and for A-flat in the key of C sing "flat-six."

Below are my suggestions for techniques you might use to hear the chromatic tones in your mind (but feel free to use whichever technique works best for you).

- For Exs. 12-1, 12-2, and 12-3, try "attaching" the chromatic tones to neighbors.

- For Ex. 12-4, use the chromatic scale to sing passing chromatic tones.

- For Exs. 12-5 through 12-10, use either "attaching to a neighbor" or singing a portion of the chromatic scale, depending on the note in question.

- For Ex. 12-11, borrow from the minor scale in measure 8; for measures 5, 7, and 10, "attach" the chromatic note to a neighbor.

- For Ex. 12-12 (in the key of E-flat), begin thinking in a new tonic (B-flat) at measure 5. In the example, both keys are represented in the legend. Scale degrees are indicated under the notes of the song *in the key you should be thinking in.*

- For Ex. 12-13, use intervals in measures 9 and 10. Note that the interval in measure 10 is a descending diminished 4th (which sounds the same as a major 3rd). Alternately, for those two bars you might pretend that you're momentarily in the key of C minor (using the C harmonic minor scale); that is, think of the first note of bar 9, G, not as "6" in B-flat major, but "5" in C minor. For the remainder of the song, "attach" the chromatic tones to neighbors.

Ex. 12-1

Ex. 12-2

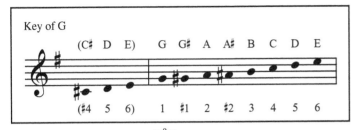

Swing feel (♫ = ♪³♪)

Ex. 12-3

Ex. 12-4

Ex. 12-5

Ex. 12-6

Ex. 12-7

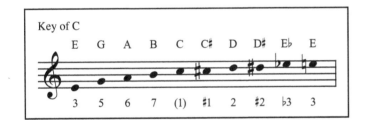

Ex. 12-8

Ex. 12-9

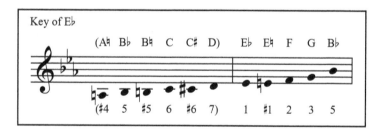

Ex. 12-10

Ex. 12-11

Ex. 12-12

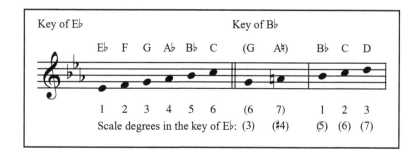

Ex. 12-13

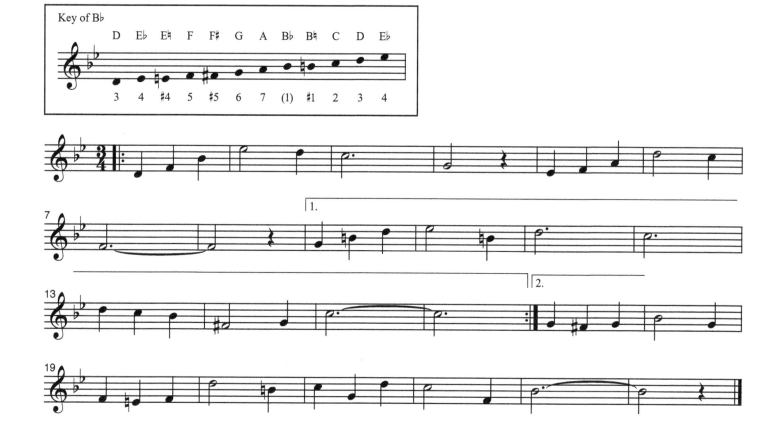

Establishing the Key (at Piano or Solo Instrument) for All Major and Minor Keys

Establishing Major Keys at the Piano

Ex. A-1

Establishing Minor Keys at the Piano

Ex. A - 2

Establishing Major Keys at a Single-Line Instrument

Ex. A-3

Establishing Minor Keys at a Single-Line Instrument

Ex. A-4

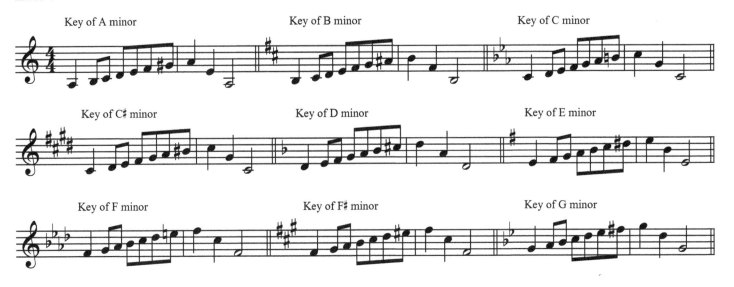

APPENDIX B:
MAJOR AND MINOR SCALES IDENTIFIED BY LETTER NAME AND SCALE DEGREE

Note: The range of these scales is two octaves, starting from G (or G♯) below middle C. The songs and exercises in this book generally don't extend beyond that range. Notes below the initial appearance of the tonic are shown in parentheses. The first note of each new (higher) octave is shown in parentheses as well.

Major Scales

Ex. B-1

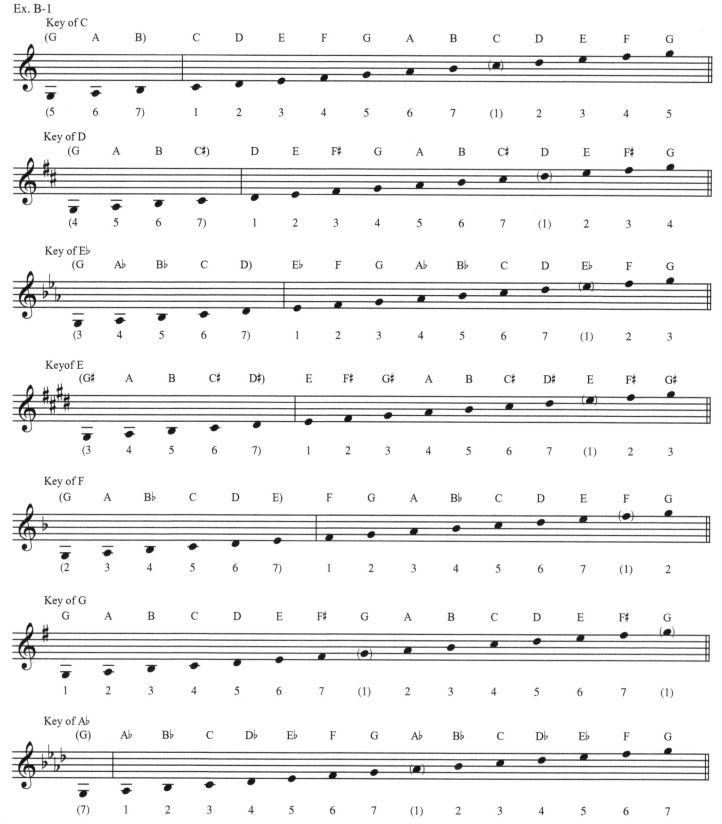

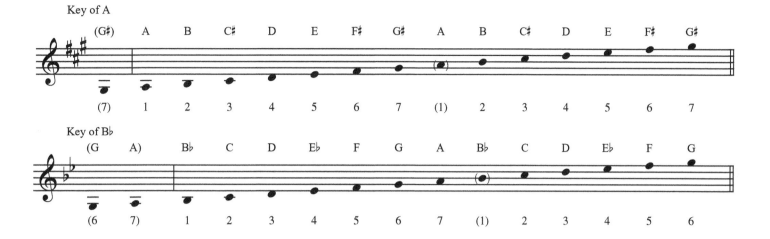

Natural Minor Scales

Ex. B-2

(Ex. B-2 cont.)

Key of F minor

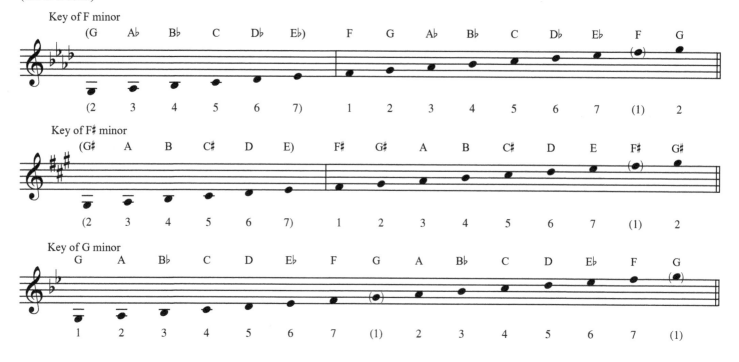

Key of F# minor

Key of G minor

APPENDIX C:
INTERVALS

A Word About Interval Terminology:

An interval is a musical distance (between two notes) as measured in scale degrees (or in consecutive musical letters). Therefore, the interval from any kind of C (C-flat, C-natural, C-sharp, etc.) up to any kind of D is always some type of 2nd—because counting letter names from C up to D (starting with C as 1) gives us a total of 2. Likewise, any type of C up to any type of A is some type of 6th (count on your fingers from C up to A to confirm this).

In the major scale, the intervals from the tonic up to the various scale degrees fall into two categories. Unisons (repetition of the same tone), 4ths, 5ths, and octaves are called *perfect* intervals; 2nds, 3rds, 6ths, and 7ths are called *major* intervals. Therefore, C up to D is a *major* 2nd; C to E is a *major* 3rd; C to F is a *perfect* 4th (often called simply a "4th"), C to G is a *perfect* 5th (or simply a "5th"); C to A is a *major* 6th, C to B is a *major* 7th, and C up to C is *perfect* octave (or simply an "octave").

If a major interval (2nd, 3rd, 6th, or 7th) is decreased in size by one chromatic half step (that is, the accidentals are altered but the letter names remain the same), it becomes a *minor* interval. For example, while C up to E is a *major* 3rd, C up to E-flat is a *minor* 3rd.

If a perfect or a minor interval is decreased by a chromatic half step it becomes a *diminished* interval. For example, C up to G is a perfect 5th, but C up to G-flat is a *diminished* 5th; likewise, C up to B-flat is a minor 7th, but C up to B–double flat is a *diminished* 7th.

If a perfect or a major interval is increased by a chromatic half step it becomes an *augmented* interval. For example, C up to F is a perfect 4th, but C up to F-sharp is an *augmented* 4th; likewise, C up to D is a major 2nd, but C up to D-sharp is an *augmented* 2nd.

Ex. C-1 shows all the common intervals in both their ascending and descending forms (with middle C as the lower note). Ex. C-2 shows all the intervals (both common and uncommon) from a diminished unison through an augmented octave, along with their names and what common interval each uncommon interval sounds the same as. Also included is the number of half steps each interval is equivalent to.

Ex. C-1

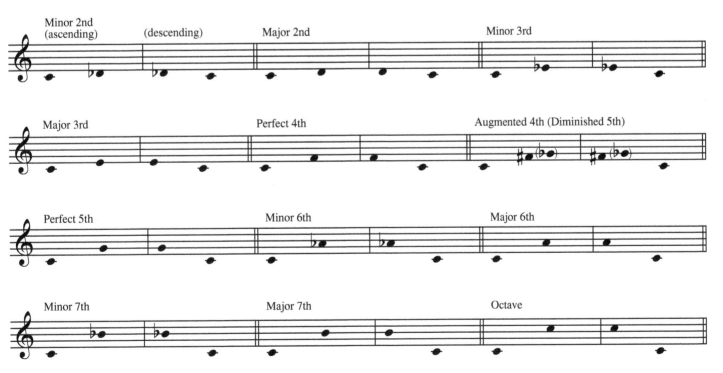

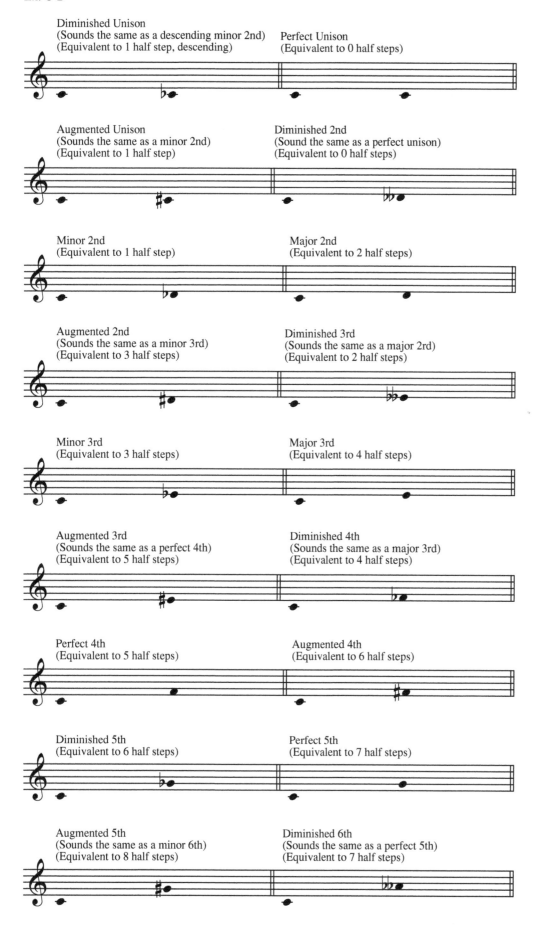

Minor 6th
(Equivalent to 8 half steps)

Major 6th
(Equivalent to 9 half steps)

Augmented 6th
(Sounds the same as a minor 7th)
(Equivalent to 10 half steps)

Diminished 7th
(Sounds the same as a major 6th)
(Equivalent to 9 half steps)

Minor 7th
(Equivalent to 10 half steps)

Major 7th
(Equivalent to 11 half steps)

Augmented 7th
(Sounds the same as an octave)
(Equivalent to 12 half steps)

Diminished octave
(Sounds the same as a major 7th)
(Equivalent to 11 half steps)

Perfect octave
(Equivalent to 12 half steps)

Augmented octave
(Sounds the same as a *minor 9th)
(Equivalent to 13 half steps)

*Octave plus
minor 2nd

APPENDIX D:
FAMOUS SONGS FOR LEARNING EACH SCALE DEGREE

"1"
1. America (My country, 'tis of thee)
2. Clementine (In a cavern, in a canyon)
3. The Christmas Song (Chestnuts roasting on an open fire)
4. Do-Re-Mi (Doe, a deer, a female deer)
5. Frère Jacques
6. I've Been Working on the Railroad
7. Kumbaya
8. Michael, Row the Boat Ashore
9. Oh, Susanna (Oh, I come from Alabama)
10. Old MacDonald Had a Farm
11. On Top of Old Smoky
12. Over the Rainbow (Somewhere over the rainbow)
13. Row, Row, Row Your Boat
14. Take Me Out to the Ball Game
15. Twinkle, Twinkle, Little Star
16. Yankee Doodle (Yankee Doodle went to town)

"High 1"
1. Beautiful Dreamer
2. Born Free
3. Hallelujah Chorus
4. Joy to the World
5. Soldier Boy—1962 hit by the Shirelles

"2"
1. Yesterday
2. People
3. Last two words of "The Star Spangled Banner" (*the* brave)
4. Last two words of "The Twelve Days of Christmas" (*pear* tree)

"3"
1. Angels We Have Heard on High
2. Brahms' Lullaby (Lullaby and goodnight)
3. By the Light of the Silvery Moon
4. Drink to Me Only with Thine Eyes
5. The First Noel
6. I Left My Heart in San Francisco
7. Mary Had a Little Lamb
8. Nobody Knows the Trouble I've Seen
9. O Holy Night (O holy night, the stars are brightly shining)
10. O Little Town of Bethlehem
11. Old Folks at Home (Way down upon the Swanee River)
12. Rock-A-Bye, Baby (Rock-a-bye, baby, on the tree top)
13. Swing Low, Sweet Chariot
14. Three Blind Mice
15. White Christmas (I'm dreaming...)

"4"

1. Last phrase of "The Birthday Song" (*happy* birthday to you)
2. Last phrase if "God Bless America" (*my* home sweet home)
3. Jennifer Juniper—1968 hit by Donovan
4. Shine On Harvest Moon

"5"

1. America, the Beautiful (O beautiful for spacious skies)
2. The Battle Hymn of the Republic (Mine eyes have seen the glory)
3. A Bicycle Built for Two (Daisy, Daisy, give me your answer, do)
4. The Caissons Go Rolling Along (Over hill, over dale, as we hit the dusty trail)
5. Camptown Races (Camptown ladies sing this song)
6. Deck the Halls
7. He's Got the Whole World in His Hands
8. London Bridge
9. Over the River and Through the Woods
10. Rudolph the Red Nosed Reindeer
11. Sailing, Sailing (Sailing, sailing, over the bounding main)
12. Sing a Song of Sixpence
13. The Star Spangled Banner (O say can you see)
14. This Old Man (This old man, he played one)
15. You're a Grand Old Flag

"low 5"

1. Amazing Grace (Amazing grace, how sweet the sound)
2. Auld Lang Syne (Should auld acquaintance be forgot)
3. Give My Regards to Broadway
4. Here Comes the Bride
5. Home on the Range (Oh, give me a home)
6. It Came Upon a Midnight Clear
7. Love Me Tender
8. O Christmas Tree
9. The Twelve Days of Christmas (On the first day of Christmas)
10. We Wish You a Merry Christmas

"6"

1. I Dream of Jeanie with the Light Brown Hair
2. I Want to Hold Your Hand (Oh yeah, I...)
3. Three Coins in the Fountain
4. To Sir, with Love (Those schoolgirl days...)—1967 hit by Lulu
5. Wonderful, Wonderful (Sometimes we walk...)—1957 hit by Johnny Mathis

"7"

1. (High "7") Don't Let the Sun Catch You Cryin'—1964 hit by Gerry and the Pacemakers
2. (Low "7") Danny Boy (Oh, Danny boy)

APPENDIX E:
ANSWERS FOR "NAME THAT TUNE"

7-1. America, the Beautiful
7-2. Auld Lang Syne
7-3. Clementine
7-4. Here Comes the Bride
7-5. Home on the Range
7-6. I've Been Working on the Railroad
7-7. It Came Upon a Midnight Clear
7-8. Love Me Tender
7-9. Michael, Row the Boat Ashore
7-10. Old MacDonald Had a Farm
7-11. Over the River and Through the Woods
7-12. Rock-A-Bye, Baby
7-13. She'll Be Comin' 'Round the Mountain
7-14. Swanee River (Old Folks at Home)
7-15. Swing Low, Sweet Chariot
7-16. Take Me Out to the Ball Game
7-17. The Twelve Days of Christmas
7-18. Twinkle, Twinkle, Little Star
7-19. We Wish You a Merry Christmas
7-20. Yankee Doodle
7-21. You're a Grand Old Flag